Broke

The Consumerism Paradox

Cory Mellor

Chapter 1: The Allure of Consumerism
In this chapter, we explore how consumerism has become deeply ingrained in American society, enticing individuals to spend beyond their means in pursuit of a desirable lifestyle.

Chapter 2: The Rise of Credit Culture
Delving into the history of credit, we examine how easy access to credit cards and loans has fueled consumer spending, masking the true financial status of many Americans.

Chapter 3: The Debt Trap
This chapter reveals the detrimental effects of mounting consumer debt, highlighting how it hampers wealth accumulation and keeps individuals in a cycle of financial struggle.

Chapter 4: Advertising and Manipulation
Exploring the psychology of advertising, we uncover how sophisticated marketing techniques exploit consumer desires and drive excessive spending.

Chapter 5: Materialism and Social Pressure
We discuss how societal expectations and peer pressure encourage individuals to keep up with materialistic trends, often leading to financial instability.

Chapter 6: Rising Cost of Living
Analyzing the cost of essentials like housing, healthcare, and education, we illustrate how increasing expenses contribute to financial strain on American households.

Chapter 7: Disproportionate Wealth Distribution
Examining wealth inequality, this chapter explains how a small percentage of the population hoards a significant portion of the nation's resources, leaving many struggling to make ends meet.

Chapter 8: Consumerism and Environmental Impact
We discuss the environmental consequences of consumerism, shedding light on the unsustainable practices associated with excessive consumption.

Chapter 9: The Illusion of Happiness through Possessions
Delving into the pursuit of happiness, we explore how material possessions often fail to provide the long-lasting fulfillment that consumerism promises.

Chapter 10: Breaking Free from Consumerism
Offering solutions and alternatives, we present strategies for individuals to escape the clutches of consumerism and work towards financial stability and true contentment.

Chapter 1

The Allure of Consumerism

In the land of plenty, where the shelves are stocked and advertisements beckon, a culture of consumerism has taken root, promising a life of luxury and fulfillment. It whispers to us through glossy ads, social media, and the very fabric of our society. It tells us that happiness and success can be found in the acquisition of things—beautiful homes, flashy cars, the latest gadgets, and designer fashion.

Consumerism has become a powerful force, shaping our desires and dictating our spending habits. It tantalizes us with visions of a life beyond our current means, fueling a perpetual desire for more. We are enticed by the idea that possessing more will make us happier, more successful, and more admired.

Advertisements bombard us daily, carefully designed to manipulate our emotions and convince us that we lack something essential, something that can only be filled by purchasing a particular product. The allure is crafted to make us believe that our lives are incomplete without the latest smartphone, the trendiest fashion, or the most luxurious vacations.

Consumerism not only seduces us into overspending but also subtly convinces us that our value and identity are tied to what we own. We find ourselves caught in a cycle, constantly chasing the next purchase, struggling to keep up with the ever-changing standards set by society.

The ease of credit and the availability of loans have further deepened this consumerist culture. It's all too tempting to live beyond our means, to finance our desires with borrowed money, creating a facade of affluence while drowning in debt.

Yet, as we chase these material dreams, the cost becomes evident. Many Americans find themselves trapped in a cycle of debt, working tirelessly to pay off what they owe, only to accumulate more. The promise of a better life through consumerism often leads to financial strain, stress, and the inability to save for the future.

In this book, we will unravel the layers of consumerism, examining its roots, its pervasive influence on our lives, and the paradox it presents. We'll delve into the intricacies of this cultural phenomenon and shed light on the ways it keeps so many Americans financially constrained, struggling to escape its grasp.

Chapter 2
The Rise of Credit Culture

In the annals of American economic history, a significant transformation occurred—a metamorphosis that reshaped the financial landscape and influenced consumer behavior profoundly. This transformation was the rise of the credit culture.

In the mid-20th century, credit cards emerged as a convenient financial tool, initially offered by department stores and gasoline companies. However, the true turning point came in the 1970s with the introduction of universal credit cards, like Visa and MasterCard, making credit easily accessible to the average citizen.

The allure of credit was undeniable. It provided a newfound flexibility in spending, allowing people to defer payments and carry balances. This flexibility was marketed as a convenience, an opportunity to enhance one's lifestyle without immediate financial strain.

Soon, the notion of "buy now, pay later" became ingrained in the American psyche. Credit cards, once a convenience, evolved into a symbol of status and prosperity. The more credit cards one had and the higher the credit limits, the more affluent one seemed. Advertisements further fueled this perception, portraying the credit lifestyle as the epitome of success and happiness.

Financial institutions capitalized on this shifting mindset, aggressively promoting credit card usage and extending credit to a broader audience. They employed enticing marketing strategies, often targeting young adults and college students. Credit cards were promoted on college campuses, enticing students with freebies and low introductory interest rates.

The financial industry refined their strategies, implementing intricate algorithms to determine creditworthiness and tailor offers. The ease of obtaining credit grew, masking the potential risks and luring consumers into a debt cycle.

However, what appeared to be a boon was, in reality, a double-edged sword. The convenience of credit often led to reckless spending, blurring the lines between wants and needs. Debt, once incurred, accrued interest, turning small balances into significant financial burdens.

In this credit-centric society, a toxic social norm emerged, weaving itself into the fabric of everyday life— the obsession with the credit score. The credit score, initially a tool for lenders to assess creditworthiness, became an emblem of societal standing.

For the poor and the middle class, the pressure to maintain a high credit score became a suffocating burden. People began to define their worth by this three-digit number, and societal validation often hinged on its stature. A lower credit score could lead to feelings of inadequacy, shame, and exclusion.

Individuals would bend over backward to keep their credit scores pristine, often at the expense of their financial stability. The fear of damaging their creditworthiness led to avoiding essential actions, like seeking necessary medical help, challenging unfair charges, or pursuing higher education, all of which might impact the score.

In my years working in the airline industry I have met many walks of life that were never taught any good financial advice, many of these individuals, drowning in the quicksand of financial desperation, resorted to unimaginable measures. They stooped so low as to exploit the innocence of their own offspring, using their young children's social security numbers to apply for new credit cards. And justify it by explaining how it will build up their credit score. The unfortunate reality is that these individuals are bad with money to begin with and end up building up the debt to an unmanageable amount. This twisted act not only destroyed the children's financial futures before they could even fathom the concept of work, but it also left a scar on their lives that would take years to heal.

We all must shed light on this pivotal transformation in American financial behavior. The rise of the credit culture altered the way people viewed and managed their finances, setting the stage for a cycle of debt that continues to impact individuals and families across the nation. Moreover, it exposed the toxic obsession with credit scores, a societal metric that has distorted priorities and hindered the pursuit of genuine financial well-being.

Chapter 3
The Debt Trap

In the grand theater of consumerism, where desires pirouette and spending takes the center stage, a menacing specter lurks in the shadows—the insidious cycle of debt.

As credit became more accessible and consumerism continued to flourish, debt began to weave itself into the fabric of everyday life for countless Americans. It started subtly, often with what seemed like manageable balances—perhaps a credit card for unexpected expenses or a car loan to afford reliable transportation.

Initially, the allure of easy credit masked the underlying dangers. Individuals, enticed by the promise of instant gratification, found themselves entranced in a spiral of borrowing. A shopping spree here, a luxurious vacation there—it all seemed manageable in the moment.

However, the ease with which credit could be obtained often concealed the impending consequences. Monthly payments multiplied, each one adding to the next, gradually evolving into a relentless debt avalanche. Interest rates, initially overlooked, compounded the burden, making it increasingly difficult to escape the clutches of indebtedness.

For many, debt began to dictate their financial decisions, affecting their ability to save, invest, or plan for the future. The weight of repayments bore down, often leading to a cycle of borrowing to make ends meet, perpetuating a vicious circle.

The situation worsened for the already financially vulnerable—those struggling to make ends meet, living paycheck to paycheck. They were more susceptible to accumulating debt, often relying on credit cards or loans to cover basic necessities when their income fell short.

Creditors, with their alluring offers and tempting schemes, preyed on the vulnerabilities of these individuals, trapping them in a relentless cycle. As the debt grew, so did the stress and anxiety, permeating every aspect of their lives.

In this debt-fueled world, the promises of prosperity and happiness were overshadowed by the grim reality of financial enslavement. Dreams were deferred, opportunities lost, and the pursuit of a stable and secure future seemed an elusive mirage.

unraveling the tale of the debt trap, exposing how the enticing allure of credit and consumerism ensnared countless Americans in a cycle of financial struggle. It delves into the devastating impact of debt on individuals and families, exploring the psychological and economic toll it exacts. Ultimately, it underscores the urgent need to break free from this cycle and seek a path toward true financial well-being.

Chapter 4
Advertising and Manipulation

In the modern era, a sophisticated art form has emerged, captivating audiences and shaping desires—the art of advertising. With its persuasive techniques and emotional resonance, it has become a formidable force, influencing consumer behavior on an unprecedented scale.

Advertisements have evolved from simple product promotions to intricately crafted narratives, carefully designed to tap into human psychology. They evoke emotions, create fantasies, and promise a better life—all through the acquisition of products and services.

In the realm of consumerism, advertisements play a starring role. They glamorize possessions, presenting them as essential to happiness and success. The airwaves, billboards, and digital spaces are adorned with images of perfect lives, painted with the brushstrokes of material abundance.

The clever interplay of colors, images, and words in advertisements triggers our subconscious desires. Advertisers adeptly exploit psychological principles, creating a sense of urgency or scarcity to provoke impulsive purchases. They tap into our fears and aspirations, creating a narrative that we lack something vital, something that their product can fulfill.

Celebrity endorsements are a potent tool in this realm, turning famous personalities into influential agents of desire. The allure of celebrities can make us aspire to their lifestyle, nudging us to emulate their choices in fashion, technology, or lifestyle, unwittingly fueling the cycle of consumerism.

Furthermore, targeted advertising, driven by data analytics, tailors messages to specific demographics, maximizing their impact. Advertisements follow us online, reflecting our interests and preferences, subtly convincing us that the products they promote are precisely what we need.

In this age of omnipresent advertising, distinguishing genuine needs from manufactured desires has become increasingly challenging. The lines between necessity and indulgence blur as advertisements coax us into purchasing more, nudging us Into a perpetual quest for the next acquisition.

The art and science behind advertising, illustrating how it molds our perceptions, influences our desires, and guides our purchasing decisions. It exposes the subtle mechanisms used to manipulate consumer behavior and calls for a critical evaluation of the messages we encounter daily. Understanding this manipulation is the first step towards breaking free from the clutches of consumerism and reclaiming control over our financial destinies.

Chapter 5
Materialism and Social Pressure

In the contemporary world, the allure of material possessions and the societal pressure to acquire them have intertwined to form a complex tapestry that shapes our values, self-esteem, and overall well-being. This chapter delves into the pervasive culture of materialism and its profound impact on our lives.

Materialism, at its core, is the preoccupation with the acquisition of goods and possessions, often viewing them as symbols of success, status, or self-worth. It fosters the belief that accumulating more wealth and possessions leads to a higher social standing and a greater sense of fulfillment.

Society has become a stage where individuals perform their roles as consumers, continually striving to display affluence and success. Peer influence, media portrayal, and cultural narratives drive this consumption-oriented lifestyle. The pursuit of material goods becomes a relentless quest for validation and recognition.

The rise of social media has exacerbated this phenomenon, creating a digital theater where people flaunt their acquisitions and curated lifestyles. The pressure to keep up with the curated images of a perfect life, perpetuated by influencers and acquaintances, can be overwhelming. Comparison and envy become persistent companions, pushing individuals deeper into the materialistic race.

Advertising, as discussed in the previous chapter, plays a pivotal role in fueling materialism. It shapes our desires and molds our aspirations, often setting unrealistic standards. We are bombarded with images of unattainable beauty, opulent lifestyles, and idealized success, igniting an insatiable appetite for more.

Moreover, the hedonistic treadmill theory posits that as we acquire more, our expectations and desires increase, leading to a perpetual cycle of consumption and discontent. The gratification derived from a new possession is often short-lived, pushing us to seek the next acquisition to maintain that fleeting sense of happiness.

The societal focus on external success, often measured by material wealth, overshadows the importance of internal values, relationships, and personal growth. As we chase possessions relentlessly, we risk sacrificing the intangible, enduring sources of true contentment.

The relationship between materialism and social pressure. It underscores the need to reassess our values, redefine success, and strive for a more balanced and fulfilling life. By challenging the pervasive materialistic narrative and focusing on what truly matters, we can break free from the shackles of consumerism and find genuine happiness and purpose.

Chapter 6
Rising Cost of Living

As the wheels of time turn, so does the cost of living, steadily and relentlessly. The sixth chapter of our journey into the complexities of consumerism brings to light a critical aspect of the modern era—the relentless rise in the cost of living.

In this fast-paced world, we find ourselves grappling with escalating prices across various essential domains of life. The cost of housing, healthcare, education, transportation, and basic utilities continues to soar, placing an ever-increasing burden on individuals and families.

However, amidst this financial challenge, a pertinent issue arises—the tendency to live beyond our means. Despite the growing cost of living, many find it difficult to adjust their lifestyle and spending habits accordingly. A culture of instant gratification and societal pressures nudges individuals to maintain a certain standard of living, even if it means diving deeper into debt.

Consumers often fall into the trap of blaming external events and circumstances beyond their control for their financial woes. Economic downturns, job market fluctuations, and unforeseen emergencies provide a convenient scapegoat for the inability to live within one's means. It's easier to point fingers at external factors than to introspect and take responsibility for our financial choices.

Rather than critically examining personal spending habits, individuals tend to use external circumstances as justification for their financial predicaments. While external factors indeed play a role, the inability or unwillingness to adjust one's lifestyle and expenses according to the financial reality exacerbates the problem.

Consumerism and societal pressure fuel this cycle. Advertisements and societal norms emphasize the need to portray affluence, pushing individuals to stretch their finances thin. The fear of falling short of societal expectations prevents them from making crucial financial decisions that prioritize stability over image.

The interplay between the rising cost of living, consumerist culture, and the difficulty of living within one's means. It underscores the importance of personal responsibility and introspection, urging individuals to reevaluate their spending habits, reassess priorities, and make informed financial choices. By looking inward and taking control of our financial decisions, we can build a more secure and sustainable financial future, even in the face of external challenges.

Chapter 7
Empowerment through Financial Mindset Shift

"If you didn't know, what you believe about the world and how it works, causes you to make decisions, those decisions affect your life." This fundamental premise underscores the power of mindset and belief systems in shaping our actions and, subsequently, our reality.

Our beliefs about wealth distribution and its impact on our lives can influence our decisions, from financial choices to career paths. If one believes that the distribution of wealth is a significant determinant of their success or failure, it may inadvertently shape their decisions and actions, potentially perpetuating a victim mentality.

However, the power lies in recognizing that money and wealth distribution are fundamentally tied to behavior. A shift in mindset from feeling victimized by circumstances to becoming a resilient, goal-driven individual, believing in one's capability to take charge of their destiny, can profoundly alter the course of their life.

This transformation is the essence of the law of attraction—the belief that our thoughts and beliefs shape our reality. By focusing on positive thoughts, setting clear goals, and believing in our ability to achieve them, we attract opportunities and circumstances that align with our aspirations.

In this perspective, the accumulation of wealth by individuals like Bill Gates or Elon Musk becomes less of a focus. Gas prices and the rising cost of living are challenges to be acknowledged, but they don't define our potential. Instead, the emphasis shifts to taking proactive steps, utilizing opportunities, and working diligently to achieve personal and financial goals.

Empowerment comes from recognizing that we are not merely passive participants in a predetermined economic landscape. We possess the agency to influence our financial destiny through conscious choices, perseverance, and a determined mindset. By acknowledging the challenges and using them as fuel for growth, we can transcend barriers and strive for success.

"What makes poor people, poor?" is a question that forces us to confront our ideologies and assumptions. It encourages self-reflection on the beliefs we hold about financial standing and wealth. By contemplating this question, we unravel societal norms, cultural expectations, and personal biases that may influence our views on poverty and success.

Asking ourselves this question fosters an understanding of the factors contributing to poverty, such as limited access to education, healthcare disparities, systemic inequalities, and economic circumstances. It challenges us to question our beliefs about hard work, perseverance, and opportunity, prompting a reevaluation of our values and the importance we place on financial security.

This introspection guides us in setting meaningful and attainable goals to avoid the mistakes often associated with poverty. By acknowledging the factors that can lead to financial struggle, we can plan effectively, striving to overcome obstacles and make informed decisions that pave the way for a more secure and prosperous future.

We are in control of our own destiny and it is up to the individual to break free from the victim mindset, shift our focus towards personal empowerment, and embrace the notion that we have the potential to shape our destiny. It urges us to rise above societal constraints, take charge of our financial journey, and make decisions that propel us towards our desired goals, regardless of external circumstances. Asking vital questions helps us critically examine our beliefs, set informed goals, and navigate our path towards financial well-being.

Chapter 8
Consumerism and Environmental Impact

Consumerism, the insatiable hunger for goods and services, has given rise to a throwaway culture that feeds on overproduction, overconsumption, and waste. Chapter 8 unravels the environmental repercussions of consumerism, shedding light on the unsustainable practices associated with excessive consumption.

In the relentless pursuit of more, our planet pays a heavy price. Mass production of goods, often fueled by non-renewable resources, generates pollution and depletes natural reserves. Factories spew pollutants into the air, water, and soil, causing irreparable damage to ecosystems and human health.

The race to meet consumer demands leads to deforestation, habitat destruction, and loss of biodiversity. Extracting raw materials for production encroaches upon critical natural habitats, displacing wildlife and disrupting delicate ecosystems. The fashion industry, for instance, contributes to habitat loss and water pollution through intensive cotton farming and dyeing processes.

Moreover, the lifecycle of products is oftentimes shorter than it should be. The rise of single-use plastics and disposable items worsens the waste crisis. Plastic waste, in particular, poses a significant threat to marine life, with millions of tons ending up in oceans each year.

The accumulation of plastic waste disrupts marine ecosystems, harming aquatic animals and impacting the food chain.

Transportation, a key component of consumerism, significantly contributes to carbon emissions and climate change. The shipping and transportation of products across the globe generate a substantial carbon footprint, aggravating environmental challenges.

Consumerism perpetuates a "fast fashion" culture, where trends change rapidly, encouraging excessive purchasing and discarding of clothing. This leads to a cycle of waste and environmental degradation. Additionally, electronic gadgets and appliances, integral to modern consumerism, contribute to electronic waste, posing a challenge in proper disposal and recycling.

The urgent need for a paradigm shift—a move towards sustainable and mindful consumption. By promoting conscious consumer choices, supporting eco-friendly products, reducing waste, and advocating for a circular economy, we can mitigate the environmental impact of consumerism.

It is crucial to recognize that each purchase we make has a footprint. By considering the environmental consequences of our choices, we can work towards a more sustainable future, striving for a balance where our lifestyles coexist harmoniously with the health of our planet.

Chapter 9
The Illusion of Happiness through Possessions

In a world driven by consumerism, we often find ourselves ensnared in the illusion that material possessions hold the key to everlasting happiness. Chapter 9 delves into the pursuit of happiness, exposing how this consumerist promise of fulfillment through possessions ultimately proves to be an illusion.

Consumerism perpetuates the myth that accumulating more, acquiring the latest gadgets, owning designer labels, or possessing a lavish lifestyle will bring us happiness. Advertisements play on our desires, suggesting that these purchases will elevate our status, garner admiration, and unlock a perpetual state of joy.

However, the reality is starkly different. Material possessions offer fleeting moments of happiness, often swiftly replaced by a desire for the next acquisition. This hedonic treadmill keeps us running in pursuit of the next possession, believing that it will provide the lasting contentment we seek.

Research in psychology and sociology consistently highlights that experiences and meaningful connections bring more enduring happiness than material goods. Our joy is often derived from memories, relationships, personal growth, and the intangible aspects of life. These elements contribute to a deeper sense of purpose and fulfillment that material possessions can rarely match.

Consumerism tricks us into believing that our worth is defined by what we own. This emphasis on material accumulation fosters a culture of comparison and competition, fueling the never-ending cycle of consumption. Our self-esteem becomes tied to external validation, perpetuating an insatiable quest for more possessions.

Minimalism and conscious consumption movements have emerged as counterpoints, advocating for intentional living and valuing experiences over things. These movements encourage us to break free from the illusion of consumerist happiness, urging us to simplify our lives, focus on what truly matters, and find contentment beyond materialism.

Chapter 9 illuminates the deceptive nature of consumerism's promise of happiness through possessions. It urges us to challenge this illusion, reevaluate our values, and seek fulfillment in meaningful experiences, relationships, and personal growth. By understanding that happiness transcends materialism, we can embrace a more genuine and enduring source of joy in our lives.

Chapter 10
Breaking Free from Consumerism

In the labyrinth of consumerism, the path to liberation and genuine contentment lies in breaking free from its grasp. Chapter 10 offers solutions and alternatives, presenting strategies for individuals to escape the clutches of consumerism and work towards financial stability and true contentment.

1. **Mindful Consumption:**
   Embrace mindful consumption by carefully considering each purchase. Ask yourself if the item aligns with your needs and values. Avoid impulsive buying and prioritize quality over quantity. Consider the environmental and social impact of your choices.

2. **Budgeting and Financial Planning:**
   Create a budget to manage your finances effectively. Track your income, expenses, and savings. Set clear financial goals and develop a plan to achieve them. Allocate funds for saving, investing, and emergency expenses.

3. **Minimalism:**
   Adopt a minimalist lifestyle by decluttering and simplifying your surroundings. Focus on owning fewer possessions that add value to your life. Prioritize experiences, relationships, and personal growth over material accumulation.

4. **Sustainable Practices:**
   Opt for sustainable products and practices that reduce your ecological footprint. Choose products made from eco-friendly materials, support local and ethical businesses, and reduce waste by recycling and upcycling.

5. **Financial Literacy:**
   Educate yourself about personal finance, investments, debt management, and retirement planning. Understand the implications of financial decisions and seek professional advice when needed. Knowledge empowers you to make informed choices.

6. **Delayed Gratification:**
   Cultivate the habit of delayed gratification by resisting impulsive purchases. Wait before making non-essential purchases, allowing yourself time to evaluate the necessity and value of the item.

7. **Community and Sharing Economies:**
   Engage in community-sharing economies by participating in local co-ops, sharing resources, or trading services. This fosters a sense of community, reduces consumption, and promotes sustainability.

8. **Financial Independence and Investing:**
   Strive for financial independence by focusing on generating passive income through investments. Diversify your investment portfolio, save for retirement,

and explore opportunities in stocks, real estate, or mutual funds.

9. **Volunteerism and Giving:**
   Find fulfillment in volunteering and giving back to society. Contribute to causes you believe in, donate to charities, and actively engage in community service. The act of giving can bring immense happiness.

10. **Self-reflection and Gratitude:**
   Take time for self-reflection, evaluating your goals, values, and motivations. Practice gratitude daily, appreciating what you have rather than focusing on what you lack. A grateful mindset cultivates contentment.

Breaking free from consumerism is a journey towards reclaiming control over your life, aligning your actions with your values, and finding genuine contentment beyond material possessions. By adopting mindful practices, embracing sustainability, and prioritizing financial literacy, you can pave the way towards a fulfilling, balanced, and financially stable future.

Conclusion

In the tapestry of modern society, consumerism has woven a compelling narrative—an enticing tale of happiness, success, and fulfillment through the acquisition of material possessions. Yet, as we journeyed through the chapters of this book, we discovered that this narrative is an illusion—a mirage that often leaves us parched, yearning for genuine contentment.

Consumerism lures us into a cycle of perpetual desire, promising joy through accumulation, only to reveal that the happiness it offers is fleeting and insubstantial. The relentless pursuit of more blinds us to the richness of experiences, relationships, and personal growth—true sources of lasting fulfillment.

We explored the financial struggles that consumerism engenders, from mounting debt to a widening wealth gap, emphasizing the importance of financial literacy and responsible consumption. We shed light on the environmental toll, urging a shift towards sustainability and mindful choices.

Yet, amid the challenges, we discovered hope—the power to break free from the chains of consumerism.

Mindful consumption, financial education, sustainable practices, and a shift in mindset towards experiences and connections offer a path to liberation.

As we conclude this exploration, we invite you to embark on a journey of self-reflection and intentional living. It is a call to challenge societal norms, question beliefs, and make conscious choices. A call to prioritize what truly matters—authentic happiness, meaningful relationships, and a sustainable future.

In this evolving narrative, you possess the quill. Write your story, one of empowerment, conscious choices, and genuine contentment. Break free from the consumerist illusions, and embrace a life where the pursuit of happiness is guided by wisdom, compassion, and a true understanding of what it means to be rich in the tapestry of existence.

www.ingramcontent.com/pod-product-compliance
Lightning Source LLC
Chambersburg PA
CBHW072223290526
45794CB00007B/2871